Apples

June Crebbin

Illustrated by Susan Hellard

CAMBRIDGE

"GET OUT OF MY ROOM!" shouts Max at
his big sister, Ruth.

"Stop shouting," says Ruth.

"DON'T TOUCH MY TOYS!" Max shouts at his baby brother, James.

"Stop shouting," says Mum.

"You're not at the market."

Granny shouts at the market. Every day,
she stands at her fruit stall and shouts,
"APPLES! LOVELY APPLES! ORANGES!
SWEET ORANGES!"

But one Saturday, Granny has a cold.
She can't shout. She can't talk. She can only
whisper.

So she goes to see Max.
Max is in bed.
"Can you come and help me at the
market?" whispers Granny.

"YES, PLEASE!" shouts Max.
He jumps out of bed. He jumps down
the stairs. He eats his breakfast quickly and
puts on his coat.

At the market, he helps Granny with the
fruit. There are lots of apples, bananas, pears,
peaches, oranges and lemons.

A man shouts, "ORANGES! SWEET ORANGES!"

"Can I shout?" says Max.

"Yes," whispers Granny.

Max picks up some apples.

"APPLES!" he shouts. "LOVELY APPLES!"

But something is wrong.

"Wait a minute," whispers Granny.

She goes to the front of the stall. She can't see Max behind the boxes of fruit. He's too small.

"That's no good," whispers Granny. She finds a box. "Stand on that."

Max stands on the box. Now he can see everyone and they can see and hear him.

He holds up the apples.
"APPLES!" he shouts. "LOVELY APPLES!"

"Four apples, please," says a lady.

She gives Max some money. Max gives her
four apples.

Then he shouts again.

"APPLES!" he shouts. "LOVELY APPLES!"

But something is wrong.

The lady is waiting.
Granny whispers, "Give her some change."
She helps him count the money.
"Thank you," says the lady.

Max stands on his box.

"APPLES! LOVELY APPLES!" he shouts.

"ORANGES! SWEET ORANGES!"

But something is wrong.

Everyone shouts louder than Max.
"APPLES! LOVELY APPLES! ORANGES!
SWEET ORANGES!"

Lots of people are buying fruit at the other stall.
But no-one is buying fruit at Max's stall.

"How can we sell all this fruit?" whispers
Granny.

Then Max has an idea.

He stands on his box.

"FREE APPLES WITH EVERYTHING YOU
BUY!" he shouts.

Suddenly, lots of people come to Max's stall.
Granny smiles.
They both work very hard!

They quickly sell everything.
Granny and Max put the empty boxes in
the van.

"Thank you for helping, Max," says Granny.
"I feel better now. Do you like selling fruit?"
Max nods – but something is wrong.

He can't shout. He can't talk.
He can only whisper.

"Oh, no," says Granny.

"Yes," whispers Max.

At home, Mum makes apple pie.
"APPLE PIE!" shouts Granny.
Max smiles. "Stop shouting,"
he whispers.